Jason, Lizzy,
– and the –
Snowman Village

CHARITY MARIE

Jason, Lizzy, and the Snowman Village

Copyright © 2020 Charity Marie

Illustration Copyright © 2020 Mikey Brooks

All rights reserved.

No part of this publication may be reproduced, distributed, or transmitted in any form or by any means, including photocopying, recording, or other electronic or mechanical methods, without the prior written permission of the publisher, except in the case of brief quotations embodied in critical reviews and certain other noncommercial uses permitted by copyright law. For permission requests, write to the publisher, via the website below.

http://www.charitymarie.com/contact

Ordering Information:

Special discounts are available on quantity purchases by corporations, associations, and others. For details, contact the publisher at the address above.

Printed in the United States of America

Second Paperback Edition

ISBN: 1-7349369-8-3
ISBN 13: 978-1-7349369-8-8

CONTENTS

CHAPTER ONE 1

CHAPTER TWO 5

CHAPTER THREE 10

CHAPTER FOUR 15

CHAPTER FIVE 21

CHAPTER SIX 29

CHAPTER SEVEN 41

CHAPTER EIGHT 52

CHAPTER NINE 61

CHAPTER TEN 70

CHAPTER ELEVEN 78

CHAPTER TWELVE 84

CHAPTER THIRTEEN 93

ACKNOWLEDGEMENTS 102

SPECIAL THANKS 104

ABOUT THE AUTHOR 107

CHAPTER ONE

Lizzy poked her head out from underneath her covers and listened, holding her breath. Everything looked big and scary in her new bedroom. Shadows lurked in the corners and crowded under the dresser. Lizzy shivered. With a quick exhale, she threw the covers back and jumped down from the bed. She raced to the door and tiptoed into the hall. She opened the door to her brother's room.

"Jay-Jay, you awake?" Lizzy whispered from the dimly lit doorway.

"Yeah," he whispered back and sat up in bed.

Lizzy tiptoed into the room and closed the door behind her. Her shadow flitted through the moonlight, and she crawled onto the bed.

"What's wrong, sis? Did you have a bad dream again?"

Lizzy shook her head. "My new room is scary. And I miss home."

"Texas is our home now."

"Don't you miss Chicago? Even a little?"

"I dunno. Maybe a little." Jason hesitated. "I do miss playing in the snow."

"Me too." Lizzy snuggled up next to him. "Do you think we'll have any snow for Christmas this year?"

Jason shrugged. "I don't think so, sis. It hardly ever snows in Texas."

"Will Santa still come if it doesn't snow?"

"Of course. It doesn't snow everywhere on Christmas."

"But what about Rudolph? He needs to guide the sleigh through the snow, right?"

Jason sat still and didn't answer for a long time. "I guess no snow just makes Santa's job easier."

Lizzy thought for a moment then sat up in excitement. "Jason, what if we make a wish for snow?"

"Oh, come on, Lizzy, that'll never work."

"If you wish on a star, it will." Lizzy slid out of the bed, grabbed his hand and tugged. "Haven't you ever heard of 'Twinkle, Twinkle, Little Star?' Come on, Jay-Jay. If we both do it, it'll definitely come true."

Jason groaned at his baby sister but let her drag him to the window.

"Okay, repeat after me." Lizzy tucked her short brown hair behind each ear then clasped her hands in front of her. She looked up into the sky for the biggest, brightest star she could find. "I wish I may, I wish I might, have this wish I wish tonight. I wish with all my might and all my heart for it to snow."

Jason repeated after her.

They stared through the window into the darkened sky. Neither moved. Lizzy barely breathed as they waited.

Jason sat back and said in a harsh voice, "I told you it wouldn't work."

Lizzy sat down with her back against the wall. "Maybe it doesn't happen right away."

"Yeah, whatever." Jason flopped onto the bed. "Go back to sleep."

Lizzy looked out the window one last time, hoping to see even the tiniest snowflake. Not seeing any, she trudged back to her room.

CHAPTER TWO

The next morning, Lizzy's voice jolted Jason from his sleep.

"Jason! Jason! Come quick!" Lizzy called from her bedroom across the hall.

He sat up, rubbing sleep from his eyes. "What now, Lizzy?"

"It's snowing!"

"Lizzy, I told you, it doesn't snow in Texas."

"No, Jason, look!" Lizzy hurried into his room and pointed at the window.

Jason walked over to the window. Even before he reached the windowsill, he saw the small pile of snow mounded against the glass. A thick blanket of white snow, untouched and sparkling in the bright sunlight, covered the backyard.

Lizzy looked at him with a smug smile. "I told you the wish would work."

"I can't believe it." He stared out the window, wide-eyed. "That wish did work! Come on, let's go!"

In the kitchen, their mother stood at the sink holding a cup of steaming coffee.

"Mom, it snowed! Can we go play?"

"I know! I can't believe it. I thought we left the snow up north when we moved here." She sighed and took a sip of her coffee.

"You have to eat your breakfast first, snow or not." She set two bowls of steaming oatmeal before them then looked out the back window. "The weatherman really got it wrong this time. He said it would be eighty degrees today."

As soon as they'd both finished and put their dishes in the sink, Jason and Lizzy looked at their mother. "Now, can we go play?"

Their mother nodded. "Just be back in time for lunch."

Lizzy hurried to pull on her bright pink snowsuit, still packed in a winter box they brought from Chicago. The arms were a little short, but her gloves made up the gap. She tugged on her boots, ignoring the pinch of her littlest toe. She flung her favorite scarf around her neck as she hurried down the stairs, Jason right behind her.

Lizzy squealed, and they ran out the front door. She immediately threw herself down on her back in a clean patch of snow and began moving her arms back and forth like she was doing jumping jacks. Carefully, she stood up in the center and looked down at the snow angel she'd just made. A clump of packed snow hit Lizzy in the shoulder. "Hey, Jay, don't do that!" Lizzy ducked from the next snowball.

"Snowball fight!" Jason announced. He threw another snowball at his little sister.

Giggling, she scooped up a handful of snow, packed it tightly, then threw it as hard as she could. "Bull's-eye!" she squealed as the snowball hit Jason in the stomach.

"I'm gonna get you for that!" Jason said.

Lizzy ran for the side of the house and around to the big backyard that led into the neighbor's field. Her breath became a vapor cloud in the air as she shrieked, running through the thick snow. She turned her head and saw Jason right behind her with his arm outstretched to catch her shoulder. Lizzy shrieked and zipped sideways out of his reach. Then he caught the hood of her coat and yanked her to the soft snow. He began tickling her.

They wrestled in the snow, Lizzy giggling and breathless. "Stop! I give. You win." She could barely speak she was panting so hard.

Jason sat up, his clothes coated in snow. "I think it's almost lunch time. I'm getting cold. Let's go home. Maybe Mom will make some hot chocolate." He stood and brushed snow off his clothes, then helped her to her feet.

"But where are we?" she asked, turning around to look back the way they'd come. Partly melted and messy snow showed where they'd wrestled but otherwise looked untouched. Nearby, Lizzy could see a small clump of trees but no houses.

"I don't know. We didn't go that far. Where's Mr. Whitmeyer's house?"

"Look over there." Lizzy pointed at a small grouping of buildings in the distance. "Maybe someone there can tell us where we are."

"Remember what Mom says. We're not supposed to talk to strangers," Jason said.

Lizzy put her hands on her hips. "Well, what do you think we should do? Do you see anywhere else we can go?"

Jason looked around. Snow stretched in all directions. His shoulders slumped. "You're right."

They walked toward the small group of white houses. As Jason and Lizzy got closer, they could see the nearest house was smaller than a normal house and had a rounded, snow-covered roof. Icicles dangled from the roof, and frost filmed the windows. Pine garlands wrapped around the porch columns. Lizzy reached out to touch the wall. It was slick like ice. A wreath made of pine boughs and brightly colored ribbons hung on the door.

"Look, Jason, a snowman. Someone lives here."

Jason stopped. "Lizzy, wait. Did that snowman just move?"

CHAPTER THREE

Lizzy stopped and stared. Her mouth dropped open as a snowman hopped toward them.

"Ahh!" the snowman yelled and tumbled over backward at the sight of them. Jason and Lizzy hurried forward to help him stand again. "How'd you two get here?"

The kids looked at each other, then back at the snowman.

"You can talk?" they asked.

"Oh." The snowman frowned; at least, it looked like he frowned. "Well, of course, I can. But what … how… what are you doing here? You're not supposed to be here!"

"Why not?" Lizzie asked.

"I … I … don't know why, but you're not! You're children, and children are not allowed." He wrung his scarf and paced back and forth. "Oh, this is bad, bad, bad. What do I do? What do I do?" The snowman stopped and stared at them. "I must get to the North Pole; there's no time to waste."

"Oh, can we come, too?" Lizzie asked. "Pretty please?

"I don't know… there's rules about these things you know," the snowman said. "Well, I can't just leave you here. You'll just have to come too." The snowman held up a small bag. From within it, he pulled out a small, yellow wooden airplane. The snowman began to wind the toy.

"What are you doing?" Lizzie asked.

"Getting our plane ready," the snowman said.

"Our plane?" Jason stepped back. "You're joking, right?"

The snowman finished winding the airplane and set it on the ground. "Step back and give it some room."

"First, a talking snowman. Now we're supposed to fly in a toy airplane?" Jason shook his head. "I must be dreaming."

Lizzie clapped her hands. "Look, it's getting bigger!"

They watched as the plane grew larger. A rope ladder unraveled down to the ground. Stubby wings extended from either side of the plane. They didn't look big enough to support the plane. A wooden propeller began to spin on the front nose.

"Hurry!" The snowman climbed the ladder and into the first seat. Lizzy looked at Jason and shrugged. He helped her climb up the side of the plane, then made his way up too.

"Seat belts, everyone," the snowman said. Once all three seatbelts clicked, a clear cover locked into place overhead.

"You're sure this thing will fly?" Jason asked, gripping the seatback in front of him. His fingers curled like claws and left indents in the seat cushion.

"Of course, I am. Now, hang on. Here we go."

The plane began to coast forward, gaining speed. Lizzy held on as hard as she could. Beside her, Jason barely breathed. The plane became lighter. They soared into the blue sky and began flying impossibly fast, straight north. Lizzy looked down. Beneath them, in all directions, the land was a bright white blur.

"Now, time for introductions. My name is Mortimer J. Coldsworth, but everyone calls me Morty. You are?"

"I'm Lizzy. This is my brother, Jason," Lizzy replied. "Why is it so important to go to the North Pole anyway?" Lizzy leaned forward, straining to hear over the rushing wind.

"Snowmen, like me, are magical creatures. Each year we awaken for two days—Christmas Eve and Christmas Day. We bring the Christmas spirit. But something is terribly wrong. We've come too early. It's only the 21st of December. It's also too warm. The Snowman Village is in danger of melting before Christmas. I'm on my way to warn Santa and ask for his help."

"Oh no!" Lizzie cried and hunched forward, pulling her coat tighter around herself. "I think it's my fault."

"How, child, could this possibly be your fault?" Morty twisted in his seat to look at her.

"My brother and I made a wish for snow last night. Then this morning, it started snowing." Lizzy hung her head and tried to hide a tear sliding down her face.

"Oh, I see. Where are you from?"

"What do you mean?" Lizzy hesitated and bit her lip. "We live in Texas."

"Texas? Oh my, you're very far from home. Isn't it normally hot there?"

"Well, it doesn't snow much," Jason said. "But it's not usually as warm as it has been lately."

"Mom says we're having one of the warmest winters on record." Lizzy clasped her hands together and stared out the window. "Mom is going to be so mad at us. We're going to miss lunch for sure."

"We can only hope Santa knows what to do." Morty pointed ahead. "Look, there's his workshop."

CHAPTER FOUR

Jason and Lizzy looked out the window of the plane. A large wooden house, looking like the most inviting place in the world, lay below. Lights shone from the windows. Sparkling snow covered rolling hills. Four smaller buildings decorated in brightly colored lights surrounded the house. Giant candy canes were scattered throughout the yard around the buildings. A large stable sat in the distance. Several reindeer stood together and looked up as the plane passed overhead.

The plane began to circle lower toward a row of flashing multicolored lights.

"Wow, Lizzy, Santa has his own landing strip," Jason said, pointing ahead.

"Yes, the only way to reach Santa's workshop is by plane" Morty replied as he steered the plane lower. A large tower stood in the distance. Below, two elves waved brightly lit beacons to guide the plane.

"It's just like at the airport," Lizzy said, leaning forward to watch as the lights got closer. Flashing lights wrapped around towering candy canes on both sides of the landing strip.

They landed with a couple small bumps and coasted to an oversized building. Elves stopped what they were doing to stare as the plane stopped before the doors.

An elf hurried out to meet them, wiping her hands on a bright red rag. Her black hair was pulled back in a bun and revealed her pointy ears and dangling Christmas tree earrings. She wore a long, red wool coat, and bells jingled with each step she took. Three bright gold stars on her coat reflected light from the nearby garland-wrapped lampposts.

"Merry Christmas, Morty. What brings you here?"

"Ginger, Merry Christmas. I must speak with Santa

right away." Morty looked over at Jason and Lizzy. "And these two could use some hot chocolate. Their tummies have rumbled practically the whole way here."

Ginger put her hands on her hips and frowned. "Now Morty, you know Santa is much too busy getting ready for Christmas. Lots to do. Surely, this can wait until after the new year. Come to think of it, why have you brought two children with you? They're not supposed to know where Santa's workshop is."

"That's part of what I've come to speak with Santa about," Morty tapped his watch. "The Snowman Village is in trouble, and we need his help."

"That sounds serious," the elf hesitated and tilted her head to look at him. "Alright then, follow me, but please be quick. We're a bit behind schedule as it is."

"Yes, yes, we'll be quick," Morty muttered and hopped along behind the elf.

Lizzy and Jason followed Ginger and Morty into the hanger. An enormous sleigh, surrounded by elves, filled the building. Lizzy watched as several elves with paintbrushes carefully dabbed paint on the sides. Short legs with bright green shoes stuck out from under the sleigh. Several elves turned and watched as they walked past. Lizzy waved and smiled.

They entered a short hallway then walked through a door into a brightly lit hallway. Off to the side, a crackling fire in the living room fireplace flickered, sending dancing shadows throughout the room. In the middle of the room, a large Christmas tree was decorated with twinkling lights, colorful balls, angels, and homemade ornaments. Lights shone from amongst the dark green branches. Mrs. Claus hurried toward them, the sweet smell of chocolate surrounding her.

"Why, hello, my dears! Merry Christmas! What brings you all here so close to Christmas?"

"So sorry to disturb you, Mrs. Claus," Morty said. "I must speak with Santa."

"He's in his workshop, of course." Mrs. Claus smiled and looked down at Jason and Lizzy over her tiny spectacles. "Would you care for some cocoa? Maybe a couple of fresh baked cookies?".

Jason and Lizzy nodded eagerly. Mrs. Claus held out a hand to each of them and led them to the kitchen. They sat at a small breakfast bar and watched Mrs. Claus as she set two steaming mugs of hot cocoa and a plate of red, green, and white decorated cookies down in front of them. Lizzy picked out one in the shape of a star and took a big bite.

"Well, Merry Christmas to you, Morty," a booming voice echoed through the room, and Santa ducked through a nearby doorway with Ginger behind him.

Jason and Lizzy froze with their cookies halfway to their mouths and stared wide-eyed. Lizzy couldn't believe her eyes. Santa was better than she had ever imagined, more real than any story could have made him. He stood so tall his head almost brushed the top of the doorway, and he had to turn sideways to fit through the door. His eyes did more than just twinkle—they shone with happiness, laughter, and love. Santa gave Lizzy a happy wink, almost as if he could hear her thoughts. She realized her mouth was hanging open and could hear her mother's voice reminding her, "Lizzy, manners!" She closed her mouth with a snap and swallowed.

"Hello, Jason and Lizzy, welcome to the North Pole." Santa looked at Morty. "Now, what's so urgent, my friend?"

"The Snowman Village is melting."

Mrs. Claus and Ginger gasped.

"Oh, my!" Santa Claus stroked his long white beard.

Lizzy spoke up in a small voice. "I'm sorry, Santa, I think it's all my fault. I wished on a star for snow." Tears filled her bright blue eyes and escaped down her cheeks.

Santa chuckled and kneeled to gather Lizzy in a hug. "Don't you worry. We'll get everything right again in no time. We'll just pay Mother Nature a visit." Santa straightened and looked at Morty. "Mother Nature should be able to cool things off enough for the Snowman Village until Christmas."

Lizzy sniffled. "Can she really help us?"

Santa laughed a deep belly laugh. "I have no doubt she can. I bet the reindeer wouldn't mind a practice run before Christmas Eve."

"Whoa, can we ride in your sleigh, Santa?" Jason asked.

"Sure you can."

"I'll get the reindeer ready, Santa." Ginger volunteered.

Mrs. Claus spoke from the kitchen doorway, "You'll want to take some things with you." She turned and began gathering items for their trip. "Let me see here. A thermos of hot chocolate, some cookies, oh, and yes, some special treats for Mother Nature, of course. There, that should do it." Mrs. Claus handed Santa Claus a bright green basket with a pretty red bow on the top. Santa leaned forward and kissed Mrs. Claus's plump cheek.

"Thank you, Mrs. Claus," Lizzy said, and they headed outside to the reindeer and sleigh.

CHAPTER FIVE

Together, Morty, Jason, and Lizzy followed Santa through his workshop. Inside, it was bright and warm. Christmas music filled the air. Colored lights and fresh garlands hung from the rafters. Small elves in brightly colored clothes and pointy hats sat in front of large workbenches making toys. Throughout the shop were stacks and stacks of wrapped presents, too many to count. Conveyor belts whizzed presents through the maze of

benches and out the side of the building. Lizzy and Jason both stopped and stared. The noise was so loud they had to shout to speak to each other.

"Lizzy, are you seeing this?" Jason asked.

Lizzy nodded, unable to speak, trying to look everywhere at once. Several elves looked up and saw Santa approaching. Elves stopped their work to wave at the group as they passed or call out a cheerful, "Merry Christmas, Santa!"

Santa, Morty, and the kids passed through the workshop and out into the cold winter air. Together, they went to the stable. Inside, elves were hooking up the last reindeer to the sleigh. Several reindeer pawed the ground and snorted; the others looked toward Santa with curiosity.

"Jason, look, it's Rudolph!" Lizzy exclaimed. Lizzy ran up to stand beside him.

Rudolph bent his head down to sniff at Lizzy's hair. Giggling, Lizzy wrapped her arms around Rudolph's neck.

"Wow, that's a surprise."

Lizzy jumped. "You can talk!"

Santa laughed. "Of course, they can. What, you thought since they could fly, they couldn't talk too?"

Jason and Lizzy laughed. "I guess so."

"We don't get many children here, as you can imagine," Santa said. Santa reached down and picked Lizzy up then swung her into the sleigh. Warm, fur-lined blankets were stacked on the seats and floor. "You'll want to bundle up tight; it might get a bit chilly."

Lizzy nodded and watched as Jason, Morty, and Santa Claus got in the sleigh.

"Ready, Rudolph?"

"Ready, Santa!" Rudolph said, quivering with excitement.

"On Dasher, on Donner and Blitzen, on one and all, to Mother Nature's forest."

As if they were one, the reindeer galloped forward. Within a few strides, the sleigh began to soar into the dark sky. Once they were airborne, Lizzy looked at the stars all around. Darkness surrounded them with only Rudolph's red nose up ahead and the bright stars above. The blankets were warm and soft, protecting them from the whipping wind. Lizzy laid her head on Jason's shoulder. Her eyes began to droop with the rocking motion of the sleigh, and soon she was sound asleep.

The sleigh flew through the night sky then gently began to descend above a dense forest before coming to rest on a grassy knoll. Santa and Morty got out of the sleigh. Lizzy opened her eyes and yawned. She nudged Jason. "Wake up; we're here."

Santa rubbed Rudolph's neck. "We won't be long, Rudolph."

"Yes, Santa," Rudolph said and turned sideways in his harness to graze.

Morty and Santa set off through the woods as Jason and Lizzy followed behind. They soon arrived at a clearing with the biggest tree Lizzy had ever seen. A small creek wound through the clearing, filling the night with the sound of running water and croaking frogs. Santa stepped up beside the tree and gave three sharp knocks. A door opened silently, and they all stepped inside. A black and white penguin waddled forward, followed by the whitest turkey Lizzy had ever seen. The penguin stopped when he saw Santa and swallowed hard as though a fish was caught in his throat.

"Hello, Santa," the penguin said. "Can we help you, sir?"

"We're here to see Mother Nature. Who are you?"

The penguin looked at the turkey next to him before he spoke again. "My name is Jonah, and this is Gary."

"I'm sorry, where are my manners? This is Mortimer J. Coldsworth," Santa said.

"My friends call me Morty," he added.

"And this is Jason and Lizzy. Will you please let Mother Nature know we're here? It's very important we speak with her as soon as possible."

"Um… yes… Mother Nature… well, you see," Jonah said, stepping back half a step. Gary and Jonah stared at the floor. "She's not here."

"Pardon me?" Santa said. "Where is she?"

Jonah giggled nervously then cleared his throat. "She's with Father Time."

"Well, where's Father Time?"

This time Gary answered. "They said something about taking a vacation to visit the history of the ages and faraway lands."

Santa looked dismayed. "Oh dear, that won't do at all. Can we reach her somehow?"

Jonah shook his head. "I don't think so. She left us in charge while she's gone."

Morty looked excited. "Maybe you can help us then."

Morty, with Jason and Lizzy's help, explained all that had happened and what they needed.

Jonah looked alarmed and flapped his flippers. "No Christmas?"

Santa nodded.

Jonah looked at Gary, who now looked very scared.

"I'm sorry," Jonah cried, "it's my fault!" He buried his head in his flippers then began to shake his head back and forth.

Gary stepped forward. "We just wanted a little more warm weather. We weren't ready for winter yet. We didn't think we'd hurt anything, honest."

Santa's eyebrows came together, and the twinkle left his eyes. "You better tell me exactly what you two are talking about."

Jonah looked up. "We turned up the temperature on Mother Nature's weather machine. Then we went to the beach to enjoy it. When we came back, we couldn't fix it." Jonah's voice increased to a wail. "And now there won't be any Christmas!"

Jason looked at Lizzy. "That explains why it's been so hot in Texas. I guess it's been hot everywhere."

Santa and Morty looked at each other.

Then Santa asked, "You're sure you can't fix it?"

Gary nodded. "We tried everything. The temperature won't budge."

"Show me," Santa said. They wound their way through the house Mother Nature built. They went down, down, down to the deepest part where the roots were. They found an enormous machine with wooden cogs, gears, and levers. Santa stood before it for a long time, stroking his snowy white beard. Jonah stood behind him with his head hung low.

Morty wrung his scarf. "Is there anything we can do, Santa?"

Santa turned away from the machine. "I'm afraid don't know how to fix it, Morty."

"Oh, dear," Morty cried. He began to twist his scarf faster. "Oh, dear."

"We must find some other way to make it cold," Santa said. They all walked back up the stairs. At the top, Santa looked at Jonah. "Have Mother Nature contact me as soon as she returns."

"Yes, Santa," Jonah said, hanging his head so low his beak almost touched his chest.

"And do not try to fix it either," Santa said, his voice stern. "You've certainly caused enough trouble."

Together, they returned to the sleigh. Santa gently snapped the reins and turned the sleigh back toward the North Pole.

CHAPTER SIX

The next morning, Jason and Lizzy awoke to the smell of fresh cocoa, eggs, bacon, and biscuits. The room was decorated like a candy cane palace from the wallpaper to the candy cane bedposts. Even the furniture was red and white like a Christmas peppermint stick. Pine green carpet covered the floor. Jason and Lizzy quickly found the kitchen thanks to directions from some elves they met in the hallway.

"Goodness me, we thought you two would sleep all day," Mrs. Claus exclaimed as she set two loaded plates down on the table loaded with food. "Come, sit and eat before it gets cold."

Santa and Morty sat at the end of the table talking quietly. Jason and Lizzy began to eat.

Mrs. Claus spoke from in front of the kitchen window, looking out over the front yard, "Santa, you better come see this."

Santa joined Mrs. Claus at the kitchen window. They watched in silence as a large, white horse with enormous wings landed in the yard.

A moment later, the door to the kitchen burst open. Everyone in the room watched as two elves entered followed by Gary and Jonah.

"Jonah, Gary, I thought I told you to stay at Mother Nature's tree," Santa said.

"We know Santa, but since we made this mess, we decided to help fix it. We left Mother Nature a note," Gary explained and ruffled his feathers.

"Right," Jonah agreed, bobbing his head. "When you make a mistake, you have to fix it."

"How did you get here?" Lizzy asked. "Neither of you can fly."

"We rode the Pegasus, of course" Gary said, as though it were the most natural thing in the world.

"The Pegasus?" Jason said and rushed to the window. "I thought those were just a myth!"

"He lives with Mother Nature and takes her wherever she needs to go."

Jason shook his head and began to laugh. Soon, he was laughing so hard, his face turned red. He tried to speak around his laughter. "Two birds… who can't fly… rode a flying horse… to Santa's workshop!"

Lizzy began to giggle as Jonah and Gary looked from Jason to Lizzy and back again.

"What's so funny about that?" Jonah asked, cocking his head. Mrs. Claus and Santa began to laugh as well.

"I suppose you get used to it after a while." Mrs. Claus wiped tears from her eyes. "You two must have flown all night. I'll find you both something to eat."

"Even if you did fly all night, you'll be going right back," Santa said, frowning at Jonah.

Morty, who hadn't moved since Gary and Jonah burst in, stared down at the table and spoke, his voice tinged with despair, "What are we going to do, Santa?"

"Wait," Gary said, "we want to help! That's why we came. Why don't we wake the Ice Dragon?"

"Gary, I told you already." Jonah flapped his flippers, annoyed. "The Ice Dragon has been asleep for years. Besides, no one knows where she went. Even if we could find her, she's more likely to think we'd make a tasty snack."

"Well, what would you suggest then?" Gary ruffled his tail feathers so hard several shook loose and floated to the floor. "Now look what you made me do!"

Jonah stepped back and looked at Santa. "I think we should talk to the abominable snowman. I bet he could help. He is made from snow after all."

"Alright you two, calm down." Santa shook his head. "The abominable snowman only *lives* in snow. He doesn't actually make snow."

Lizzy looked up from her nearly empty plate. "Could we just take snow from the North Pole to the Snowman Village? Santa's sleigh looks big enough."

"Not enough time to do that and still get ready for Christmas," Santa said.

"I know!" Jason looked up, excited. "What about a giant snow machine?"

Lizzy shook her head. "Wouldn't that take too long?"

Santa agreed. "Plus, it would take too long for one machine."

Mrs. Claus spoke next as she set plates on the table for Gary and Jonah. "Why not ask Merlin to help?"

"The wizard?" Jonah asked.

Lizzy tried to remember what she had read about Merlin. All she could remember was a story about an old man with a pointy blue hat who could use magic.

"Wait," Jason said, holding up his hand. "Are you talking about Merlin from the books about King Arthur?"

"That's the one. He retired a few years ago," Santa replied. "And now he only uses his magic to keep others away."

"He's got to be thousands of years old!" Jason exclaimed. "You're telling me he's real too?"

Santa chuckled. "Yes, as are most mythical figures. It's part of what makes us legendary."

Jason shook his head. Lizzy couldn't think of anything to say to that either. It seemed too big to imagine.

Silence filled the air as they each thought and thought. Then Lizzy said, "Wait a second, if all legendary creatures are real, then what about Jack Frost? Isn't he supposed to bring winter every year or something?"

Santa looked sharply at Lizzy. The silence hung in the air, frozen like an icicle.

"What?" she asked, looking around. "Did I say something wrong?"

Mrs. Claus put her hand on Santa's arm. "Now, sweetheart, that was a very long—"

"He almost ruined Christmas!" Santa said, his rosy cheeks turning a shade redder. "If it hadn't been for Rudolph coming along when he did, why I don't know what we would have done."

"What do you mean he almost ruined Christmas?" Lizzy asked.

Santa sighed. "I'm sure you know the song about Rudolph?"

Jason and Lizzy nodded.

"It's not just a funny song," Santa said.

Mrs. Claus interrupted him, "Years ago, Jack was head elf in Santa's workshop. Every Christmas, Jack helped make sure it never snowed too hard so it was safe to deliver Christmas presents. But one year, Jack tried to use a blizzard to stop Santa from delivering presents."

"But why would Jack Frost want to do that?" Lizzy asked and looked at Santa.

"No one is really sure," Santa added. "But he would have succeeded if Rudolph hadn't come along with his red nose. Now, Rudolph always leads the sleigh. There have been lots of other times having Rudolph lead the sleigh has saved Christmas too."

Mrs. Claus looked at Santa. "You know, dear, maybe if you talked with Jack, you could get him to help? Perhaps share a little Christmas spirit? I'm sure he's quite lonely in his ice castle all alone."

"So, Jack Frost could do it, "Lizzy said, looking at Mrs. Claus. "But you're not sure he will?"

Santa sighed. "It's not that simple, Lizzy."

"Well," Lizzy looked at Jason. "Like Mom always says, you never know until you try."

Morty nodded. "Besides, what other choice do we have?"

Santa turned toward one of the elves standing near the doorway. "In that case, let's send Merry and Franki to Mother Nature's tree. Maybe they can figure out how to fix the weather machine. It won't be easy without them in the workshop. Ginger, would you please ask Hot Rod to hook up the small sleigh and make sure Jonah and Gary go with them?"

"Yes, Santa." Ginger bowed and the three headed for the workshop.

Morty stared at Santa. "So, how are we going to convince Jack Frost to help us?"

Lizzy thought for a moment. "My mom says the best way to reach a person is through kindness. Since it's almost Christmas, maybe we should bring Jack a gift?"

Mrs. Claus smiled at Lizzy and agreed "That's a wonderful idea."

"Remember," Santa said, "a gift should only be given in the Christmas spirit, not to get something in return."

"Maybe because we thought enough to give him something, he'll want to help us," Lizzy replied.

"How about some Christmas cookies?" Jason offered. "Everybody loves Christmas cookies."

Mrs. Claus nodded. "As I recall, Jack likes frosted sugar cookies."

"Oh, can I help make them?" Lizzy asked.

Mrs. Claus laughed. "Of course!" Lizzy followed Mrs. Claus into the kitchen. As Mrs. Claus and Lizzy began to make the cookies for Jack Frost, Santa and Jason headed to the workshop.

❄ ❄ ❄ ❄ ❄

Far away, Gary, Jonah, and the elves began the descent toward Mother Nature's tree.

"You're pulling on the reins too hard, Jonah," Gary cried. "I think he's getting angry."

Pegasus tossed his head, then folded its wings flat against its body and dropped the last few feet to the ground. Jonah and Gary squawked in fear and tumbled from the back of the giant animal, landing in a heap on the ground. The sleigh and reindeer landed behind them.

"How rude!" Gary exclaimed and helped Jonah up.

Pegasus snorted at him, pawed the ground, then turned his back. His long tail whipped through the air as he lowered his head to graze on the bright green grass at his feet.

"Come on," Jonah said, making sure to stay far away from the Pegasus' hooves. They met the elves at the sleigh. Franki and Merry jumped down carrying small sacks, and they all walked into Mother Nature's house.

"My, my," Franki exclaimed, looking up at the towering weather machine. An oak staircase wound through the room, weaving a strange but beautiful pattern through the machines. A row of windows allowed light from the sun to shine in. They stared at the machine until Merry clapped her hands. "Let's get started!"

Franki picked up his small sack. "I'll take the upstairs level."

Merry looked at Gary and Jonah. "Why don't you two show me where you changed the temperature last time? We'll start there."

"This way." Gary and Jonah led the way down the center aisle, and Merry looked from side to side at the different equipment.

Soon, Gary and Jonah went around a corner as Merry stopped to study a particularly interesting lever.

"Hey, Merry," Jonah said. "I think we might have found something. It's a crank, want us to try it?

"Sure, Jonah, go ahead," Merry said, not looking up from the machine in front of her.

Jonah reached up with his flippers and gave a little hop, but he couldn't reach it. He looked over at Gary.

"Hey, don't look at me." Gary stepped back. "I've only got feathers – that's not gonna do much good."

"Oh, come on." Jonah sighed. "Give me a boost, Gary."

Gary cocked his head, gobbled a couple times, then nestled down onto the floor underneath the crank. Jonah climbed on top of him and tried to balance.

"Hold still, Gary." Jonah started to wobble.

"I am!"

Jonah stretched and stretched. Then his foot slipped on one of Gary's feathers, and he fell off, face first.

"Uh, Merry, we need a hand over here," Gary said.

Merry laughed and walked closer. "I just wanted to see if you'd try it."

"Thanks a lot," Jonah grumbled, pushing himself over onto his back. Gary stretched out his long neck to help Jonah stand.

Merry studied the crank then shrugged. "I suppose you have to start somewhere." She grunted as the wheel began to turn. "Let me know if something happens."

Gary and Jonah looked around. Jonah pointed at a nearby window. "Hey look, a rainbow." Merry stopped cranking and looked.

"Hmm, a rainbow but no rain," Merry pulled the lever next to the crank. A loud bang came from one of the windows. Then another. Jonah covered his ears with his flippers as more bangs came, one after another, growing louder. "What is that?"

Franki called down from several levels up and nearer the windows. "It's hail. And a lot of it."

"Oops," Merry said and pushed the lever back down. "That's not what we need."

She tore some yellow colored tape and stuck a small piece on the lever.

CHAPTER SEVEN

As Gary, Jonah, and the elves tried to figure out Mother Nature's weather machine, Jason, Lizzy, and Morty prepared to leave for Jack Frost's castle. Two prancing reindeer stood ready to pull along torpedo shaped sleigh. Both reindeer pranced in place like little children making the harnesses rattle and jingle.

"Can we go yet, Hot Rod?" asked one of the reindeer. Of the two reindeer, she was smaller with bright red bows

tied to her short brown antlers. She turned to look at the elf climbing out from under the sleigh.

"Not yet, Jitterbug. You'll know when it's time because I'll be sitting in the driver's seat, remember?"

Jitterbug gave a little leap pulling the reindeer beside her sideways. "Hurry up!"

"Hey, Jitterbug, quit jerking me around," the reindeer beside her cried.

"Sorry, Blue Streak," she replied.

Lizzy looked at Hot Rod. "I've never heard of Jitterbug and Blue Streak. They're not in the Rudolph song."

The tiny elf chuckled. "That's because they came after the song. Blue Streak is the son of Comet and Dasher. He's so fast none of the others can keep up. Jitterbug is the daughter of Vixen and Cupid. She's so high strung she can't keep step with the others. They're good reindeer; they just need to grow up some. And they're the only reindeer who can keep up with the rocket sleigh. We're using it to train the younger reindeer."

"Wait," Jason looked at the elf. "What's a rocket sleigh?"

Hot Rod nodded. "I invented it myself. It's still being tested, but when you've got to get somewhere in a hurry, it's the only way to go."

Jason laughed. "Just when I think I've heard of everything."

Mrs. Claus came out of the house and handed Lizzy a small tin wrapped in a bow. "Here are the cookies, dear." She then handed a green and red picnic basket to Jason. "I packed some food in case you get hungry. And of course, some hot cocoa."

Jason put the basket in the sleigh.

"Thanks, Mrs. Claus." Lizzy hugged her, her arms unable to wrap all the way around Mrs. Claus's waist.

Lizzy and Jason settled into the sleigh, as Hot Rod climbed into the driver's seat.

"Is it time now?" Jitterbug asked, cocking her head sideways to look at him.

"Yes, Jitterbug, but remember – nice and easy. Start at a trot then work up to a gallop once we're above the treetops, or you'll break the chains. Again."

"Wait," Jason cried. "What do you mean 'again?'"

"Don't worry, the sleigh has a parachute."

Jason sat back, clenching the side of the sleigh, looking a little pale. "Somehow, that doesn't make me feel any better."

"Alright, you two, on my count." Hot Rod snapped the reins. The reindeer began to prance forward in tandem, their hooves kicking up light, fluffy snow. Soon, the reindeers' eight thin legs were a blur. The sleigh began to lift and angled up into the dark sky.

Lizzy looked over the side to watch as Santa's workshop grew smaller below them.

"Ok, on three," Hot Rod cried. "One, two, three." With a roar, the rocket engine started, and the reindeers' legs couldn't be seen because they moved so fast. The force pushed Jason and Lizzy back against the seat.

"Hey, Hot Rod, what happened between Jack Frost and Santa?" Lizzy asked.

Hot Rod rubbed his chin while trying to remember something that happened a long time ago. "You know Jack Frost and Santa used to be a team, right? Then, one Christmas, there was a horrible blizzard. Santa asked Jack Frost to help, as he had always done before, but Jack refused."

"Why would Jack Frost stop helping Santa?" Morty asked.

Hot Rod shrugged. "No one really knows. Everyone loves Santa. I've always thought Jack was jealous of Santa. After all, everyone leaves cookies and milk for Santa every year. They even left carrots for the reindeer. But when was the last time anyone left anything for Jack Frost? No one ever thanks Jack for bringing the snow either. I don't think anyone has even given him a Christmas present, other than Santa."

"That's awful!" Lizzy said, looking very sad.

"But it's different," Jason said. "Jack Frost doesn't leave gifts wrapped up like Santa does. So how can you give him anything?"

Hot Rod was quiet for a moment. "I suppose you're right. Anyway, I'm sure we'll find out soon enough, Jack Frost's castle isn't too far now. Wait a second, what's that?"

Lizzy looked ahead but the sleigh was going too fast to see anything.

"Ouch," one of the reindeer cried and jerked sideways. Small hail began to fall, hard and fast, onto the rocket sleigh and reindeer. The sleigh jerked and bucked, as the two reindeer tried to dodge the stinging hail.

"Hang on," Hot Rod said and banked the sleigh to the right, trying to avoid running into the large wall of hail ahead.

Jason grabbed Lizzy and the side of the sleigh, holding on with all his might. Morty slid off the seat and onto the floor of the sleigh. They were traveling too fast and turned sideways.

The reindeer dove down, pulling the sleigh into a steep drop. Hot Rod shouted and yanked on the reins but the reindeer paid no attention. They had forgotten all about the rocket sleigh, only focused on getting away from the painful sharp ice. Golf ball sized hail began to bounce off the sleigh, leaving dents. The sleigh's cover began to crack. With a bone-jarring crash, the sleigh hit the ground, bounced several times and came to rest sideways against some trees.

"Is everyone ok?" Hot Rod asked, trembling.

"I think so," Jason said.

Hot Rod pushed back the cover, leapt to the ground, and ran to the reindeer. Both were pressed up against the tree trunks, trembling, legs curled under them. Blue Streak shielded Jitterbug from the sporadic hail that broke through the tree branches.

Jason looked down at Lizzy. "Are you ok?"

Lizzy tucked her head against his chest and hugged him. She shook from head to toe.

Jason rubbed her back. "It's ok, sis. We're ok." Lizzy wasn't sure who he was trying to convince, her or himself.

Just as suddenly as it began, the hail began to slow, the ice growing smaller and smaller until it stopped completely.

Hot Rod walked out from under the tree branches, holding his hand out to test for any falling ice. Nodding, he turned back to the sleigh then stopped and groaned. "Oh no! My poor baby!"

Jason and Lizzy stood up. The sleigh looked like it had come out the wrong side of an asteroid belt. Deep dents, scratches, and cracks covered the sleigh, marring its once bright red paint. In some places, the metal showed through the scraped paint. A few feet away, one of the sleigh's runners lay lopsided in the snow.

"This is not good." Hot Rod walked around the sleigh, touching the larger dents as though they hurt him. When he got to the rear boosters, he gripped his head in both hands and moaned as if his stomach hurt. Lizzy and Jason joined him at the back of the sleigh. Part of the booster's metal fin was gone. Inside was a jumble of mangled metal. A large hole gaped through the fin of the other. Another hole, the size of a fist was in the back end of the sleigh, where hail had punched through.

Morty hopped out of the sleigh and worked his way toward Hot Rod. "Oh, dear," he said. "Can it be repaired?"

"I don't have the equipment with me to fix it, it's back at the workshop. I need some sheet metal and a torch, at least, but the hail damaged the boosters themselves. If the hail got inside, there's no telling what damage is in there." Hot Rod stopped and leaned against the sleigh.

"Morty, what are we going to do?" Lizzy asked.

Morty shook his head. "I don't know."

Jason's stomach growled loudly and echoed in the silence of the small woods.

"Sounds like we should eat something. Maybe we'll think of something with full tummies," Hot Rod declared and climbed into the sleigh to retrieve the picnic basket. Hot Rod, Jason, and the reindeer cleared the ground free of snow, and all of them crowded around the tree. The sleigh blocked the gusting wind and created a cozy space.

Hot Rod pulled out some small sandwiches, wrapped fruit and nuts, and carrots for the reindeer. Finally, he opened the hot cocoa thermos and handed cups to Jason and Lizzy. Both eagerly cupped them in their cold hands and sipped.

The group was quiet, eating and drinking, each lost in their own thoughts.

Lizzy spoke first, "Do we have to go back to Santa now?"

Hot Rod looked at Lizzy. "It might be best. But then again, I did see Jack Frost's castle right before the hail started."

"Then maybe we should keep going?" Jason shrugged. "It's shorter to Jack Frost than it is to Santa, right? Especially without the rocket sleigh."

Morty nodded. "So how do we get there from here?"

"How far do you think it is to Jack Frost's castle, Hot Rod?" Jason asked.

Hot Rod brushed the crumbs off his pants and straightened his pointy hat. "I'll climb up a tree and see." He climbed up on Blue Streak. With a little hop, Hot Rod caught the lowest branch. Giving himself a swing, he caught the next branch and began to make his way up the tree. Soon he was so high they couldn't even see his bright yellow shoes.

Jason and Lizzy finished their sandwiches, occasionally looking back up the tree. Finally, they could hear Hot Rod carefully making his way back down. He dropped from the low branches and landed in the snow like a gymnast.

"Well?" Morty asked. "What did you see?"

"It looks pretty close. Maybe a couple hours' hike. You could probably be there before sunset if you tried."

"Wait a minute, you mean you're not coming with us?" Morty asked.

"I need to get the sleigh back to the shop. It can't stay out here. And the reindeer are going to have a hard time dragging this through the trees to a spot flat enough they can take off."

"But how are we supposed to know we're going the right way?" Morty cried. "None of us know the way!"

"No problem, just head east, and you can't miss it." Hot Rod said, petting Blue Streak's neck. "I've got a compass if you want."

"But why can't we leave the sleigh here and come back for it later?" Jason asked.

"Are you kidding? Do you have any idea what would happen if someone came across this sleigh? It would be a disaster!" Hot Rod shook his head. "No way am I leaving it out here. Not to mention, this is very sensitive and secret equipment. Wouldn't want the wrong person to get their hands on it."

Jason looked at Morty. "I guess we don't have a choice." He took the compass Hot Rod held out.

"I'll be back to get you as soon as I can," Hot Rod said.

They began to clean up from their small meal, carefully repacking the picnic basket. Hot Rod untangled the reindeer from their harnesses then climbed onto Blue Streak's back. Together, the reindeer strained and pulled the sleigh, trying to get it to sit correctly.

Once the sleigh was away from the trees, it rolled sideways and began to slide easier. Hot Rod stopped and called out to them, "Good luck! Remember, stay east, and you can't miss it." He gave a wave then a gentle nudge to Blue Streak. The sleigh began to slide once more, heading north. Jason, Lizzy, and Morty watched it disappear into the trees then began the long march toward Jack Frost's castle.

CHAPTER EIGHT

Meanwhile, at Mother Nature's tree, Gary, Jonah, and the elves still hadn't found a fix for Mother Nature's weather machine.

"I'm going to try something." Franki pulled a nearby rope and pushed a bellows at the same time. The tree began to fill with a loud whooshing sound. Gary and Jonah looked at each other, then at Merry. The whooshing sound got louder and closer.

"Look out," cried Merry. "It's a sandstorm. Run!"

Franki stopped pushing on the bellows, but the sand didn't stop.

"We've got to get out of here," Jonah shouted then coughed as he got a mouthful of sand.

Franki scooped up Gary, and Merry picked up Jonah. They ran up the stairs through blinding, swirling sand and burst out the front door of Mother Nature's tree. Franki and Merry struggled to pull the door shut behind them.

"Whew," Franki said and slid down the door until he was half laying on the ground, only his elbows keeping him up. "That was close."

"Now what are we gonna do?" Gary shook a cloud of sand from his feathers.

"Well, we have no idea how to turn the storm off. I doubt it'll stop on its own." Merry said.

"I sure hope Morty, Jason, and Lizzy are having better luck than we are," Gary looked at Merry.

Franki agreed, "I guess we have no choice but to go back to Santa's workshop."

"Don't leave us here," Jonah and Gary cried together.

Jason and Lizzy stared at the sheet of ice ahead of them. It softly crackled as if trying to speak. "Morty, are you sure this is the right way?"

"The compass says this is east." Morty edged out onto the ice, testing the sturdiness. He gave a couple hops, and the ice stayed firm. "Looks safe."

"There's just one problem," Jason said. "We can't walk on ice."

"Ah, yes, excellent point." Morty pulled a small sack from between his layers of snow. Reaching inside, he fished around, feeling for something.

"What's that, Morty?" Lizzy asked.

"It's just a gift sack. A magic one, of course."

"What does it do?" Jason asked.

"It will pretty much give me anything I need based on what I picture in my mind," Morty said.

"What?" Jason exclaimed, "Why didn't you tell us this before?"

"Uh," Morty paused. "I don't know. I didn't think of it. There are some limits, I guess. It does need to be toy-related. No food, dangerous things, or anything like that."

"What are you picturing?" Lizzy asked, looking puzzled.

Morty chuckled. "Ice skates."

Lizzy looked sad. "But Morty, I don't know how to ice skate."

Morty paused and pulled a pair of skates from the bag. "Jason, do you know how to skate?"

Jason nodded.

Morty handed the skates to him. "These will fit themselves to your feet. I will wish for a sled. Then Jason and I can pull you across the ice."

Lizzy clapped her hands with delight. "That sounds like fun."

Morty pulled a bright red sled from his bag and set it on the ground before Lizzy. A yellow rope dangled from the end. Lizzy climbed onto it and put the picnic basket next to her. Jason picked up the rope. Morty took the lead, checking the ice carefully to make sure it would hold. Together, they worked their way across the slick ice, squinting against the sunshine reflecting up at them. For a long time, no one spoke. The only sound was the swishing of Jason's skates and the sled as they moved across the ice.

"How much further, Morty?" Jason asked.

"I'm not sure. I still don't see anything but ice up ahead."

"I hope it's soon," Lizzy said. "I'm starting to get really hungry."

"Me too," Jason said. "You're sure you can't wish for some food Morty?"

"I'm afraid not. But it can't be too far, right? We've been walking for hours."

A light snow began to fall, flakes lazily drifting down from the sky. The sun disappeared behind clouds, and the sky became overcast and gray.

"Morty, what does Jack Frost look like?" Lizzy asked.

"Hmm... let me see. I've only met him once, a long time ago when I was a young snowman. I remember him being very thin and tall, but that's about it. I hear his skin is cold to the touch like ice runs in his veins instead of blood. Which, if that's true, would explain why he rarely ever leaves his castle."

"Where did Jack Frost come from?" Lizzy gripped the sled rails as they slid down a little hill.

"That's an interesting story," said Morty. "Many years ago Mother Nature called a meeting with Santa and the other magical creatures. As the story goes, Santa, Merlin the wizard, the Ice Dragon, and Frosty the Snowman, then Elder of the Snowman Village, gathered to give magic abilities to Santa's top helper, Jack. Each person gave a little magic in the ceremony. Of course, it couldn't be just any helper, but one with integrity and strength. So, they decided to give Jack the power to control cold weather.

At the time, not everyone agreed with giving magic to anyone who didn't naturally have it. Merlin the wizard didn't want to help, but Mother Nature said he must. Merlin was worried about what that much power would do to a fragile elf's soul, particularly since Jack volunteered.

Not long after Jack received his powers, Merlin retired from magic. The Ice Dragon found an ice cave and refused to return to the surface. And of course, we all know what happened to Frosty."

"Wow, there must've been a very big problem for them to need to give Jack magic powers," Jason said.

"Yes, there was a big problem for Santa… "

"Look, trees!" Lizzy said, pointing ahead. Snow lay in rounded heaps. At the edges, the ice ended, and frozen ground was visible.

"We made it!" Jason said and skated forward to the snow bank.

"How much farther do you think it is, Morty?" Lizzy stood in the sled and stretched then jumped into the snow.

"We must be getting close."

"I hope so. I'm so hungry," Jason said, rubbing his stomach. "And cold. Let's stop and rest for a minute."

Together, they wiped snow off a nearby fallen tree and sat to catch their breath. Jason removed his ice skates and picked up the picnic basket. He pulled out the wrapped box and said, "Hey, what's this?"

"Christmas cookies are in there," Lizzy yanked the box away. "Those aren't for you, Jason."

"But I'm starving. Can't I have just one?"

Lizzy leaned toward Jason. "They're for Jack Frost, remember? See there's even a tag saying, 'For Jack.'"

"He won't miss just one tiny cookie," Jason said.

Lizzy clutched the box to her chest as though it would break. "Yes, he will. Plus, that's not in the Christmas spirit. Come on, let's keep going." Lizzy carefully returned the box to the basket.

"Easy for you to say," Jason grumbled under his breath as he stood. "You were dragged the whole way here. I worked up an appetite!"

Lizzy ignored him and trudged through the snow, following behind Morty. Morty did his best to block the wind but it whipped around him, stinging her ears and cheeks. "It's getting dark, Morty," Lizzy stopped at a nearby tree to rest. "Are you sure we're going the right way?"

Morty looked at the compass. "We're still heading east. Haven't strayed at all."

"Maybe Hot Rod was wrong?" Lizzy bit her lip and looked toward the horizon. "Maybe Jack Frost's castle wasn't as close as he thought?"

Morty stared to the east, looking for any sign of the castle. "Let's just hope it's over that next hill."

Jason picked up some snow and let it fall. "What if we don't find it before nighttime, Morty? We can't sleep in the snow."

Morty looked at the ground and didn't speak for a moment. "I guess we'd need to find some shelter somehow. Or else, go back to Santa's workshop." They all fell silent until Lizzy spoke, her voice soft.

"But if we can't get to Jack's castle, there won't be any Christmas."

Morty hung his head. "Yes, and it would be the first time. Ever. I would never be able to go back to my village."

"Then we can't give up. We just have to find a way." Lizzy stood and looked up at the tree. "Hey Jason, could you climb up and see if we're close?"

Jason looked up at the tree branch above his head. "I could try. But I can't reach."

Morty stood. "Here, let me help you. I could be able to lift you high enough."

Using the tree for balance, Jason climbed up Morty's back, dislodging small puffs of snow. Morty grimaced with each step Jason took. He went as high on Morty as he could then Jason stretched to reach the branch but it was just too far.

"I can't reach. I'm still too short." Jason slumped then jumped down into the snow. Lizzy picked up snow and loosely packed it then used it to patch the holes left behind in Morty from Jason's shoes. A distant growl of thunder sounded above the whipping wind, and Lizzy jumped.

"Oh dear," Morty said, looking to the west, in the direction they had come. Fast-moving, dark gray clouds appeared in the distance and grew closer as they watched.

"That's not good," Jason said.

A loud crack of thunder sent a vibration through the air, and Lizzy shrieked.

"Morty, we better find Frost's castle. Quick," Jason said.

CHAPTER NINE

The three of them labored up the hill's steep slope. The deep snow and Lizzy's short legs made it hard for her to walk on her own, so they all held hands. Jason helped pull Lizzy along beside him, both of them panting for breath. The sun disappeared behind the angry-looking gray clouds. The world around them filled with shadows.

A loud boom of thunder cracked overhead. Lizzy fell to her knees in the snow. She covered her eyes with her gloved hands, and her shoulders shook.

"Lizzy, what's the matter?" Jason cried. He tried to pull her arms away from her face.

Lizzy looked up at him. Her face was red and streaked with tears. "Th-th-thunder."

"Oh my gosh, I forgot," Jason said and wrapped his arms around Lizzy. She buried her face in his shoulder, shaking from head to toe so hard Lizzy thought she might fall over again. "Morty, she's terrified of thunder."

"Then she probably doesn't like the lightning either, huh?"

Jason shook his head and lifted Lizzy's head from his shoulder so he could look at herface.

"Lizzy?" Her blue eyes, wide and teary, stared up at him. "I need you to listen, okay?"

Lizzy nodded, her eyes never leaving his.

"The next time you hear thunder, I want you to count until it ends. Can you do that?"

She nodded.

"I'm going to be right here with you, holding your hand. You can squeeze my hand as tight as you want if you're scared. Remember, thunder can't hurt you."

"You're sure?" she asked, looking up at the clouds.

"I'm positive," he said and helped her stand. "Just hold

onto my hand. We're going to outrun this storm, what do you say?"

Lizzy nodded, biting her lip. Hand in hand, they ran up the hill, snow flying in every direction. Another loud boom of thunder sounded right overhead, rolling through the clouds. Lizzy froze and squeezed her eyes shut tight, as tears ran down her face. She squeezed Jason's hand and forgot to breathe. Finally, the thunder stopped. Jason looked down at Lizzy. "Okay?"

Lizzy took a deep breath, her face still wet with tears but she nodded. "I counted to five."

"Okay, let's keep going." Each time the thunder rolled through the sky, they stopped until the sound faded. Then, they arrived at the top of the hill. At the base of the next hill, they could see Jack Frost's castle.

"Lizzy, you did it!" Jason said, picking her up in a big hug.

Lizzy grinned. Relief cleared the tears from her eyes, and she hugged him back.

"I can't believe it." Lizzy danced around in the snow. "We did it. We really did it!" She looked up at the menacing clouds above them.

"You don't scare me anymore!" she yelled as loud as

she could. She laughed as Jason twirled her through the air. In response, the clouds gave a short bark of thunder. This time Lizzy didn't even jump.

Morty led the way down to Jack Frost's castle. As they reached the bottom of the hill, Jason and Lizzy stopped and stared, taking in the amazing scene before them. In every direction, tall trees stretched above their heads. Perfectly carved in ice were leaves, branches, even the bark. The trees were close enough together their branches connected, creating an icy canopy. Multicolored light shone through as if being put through a prism. Light danced among the frozen landscape as the ice sang its own beautiful song, crackling and tinkling in celebration.

"Oh, my gosh, Jason!" Lizzy said, breathless. "It's so pretty!"

Jason nodded without taking his eyes off the ice above them. "I just hope it's safe."

Morty turned to them. "If we're going to keep from getting wet, we better keep moving."

As he spoke, the ice's song changed its rhythm and became faster like the tinkling of many tiny bells. They all looked up above them in wonder as a soft drizzle fell onto the ice and slid a short way before freezing solidly in place.

"Wow!" Jason reached out for Lizzy's hand. Hand in hand, they walked through the ice forest, looking all around.

"Jason, look, it's a deer peeking through the trees." Lizzy pointed. "It's made of ice too."

"There are birds in the trees too," Jason said. "That one even has its wings spread."

The group made its way through the wintry wonderland until they arrived at a clearing. An enormous door blocked their path. Morty hopped up and gave the handle a good tug. It didn't budge.

"Uh oh." Jason tried the door too. "This is not good. It's locked."

"Great." Lizzy kicked the snow in front of her. "All this way to be stopped by a stupid locked door. Now, what are we gonna do?"

"I suppose we could knock?" Morty said.

Jason shrugged and knocked as hard as he could on the ice-covered door. The knock died off without reaching past their ears.

"That's not going to work," Jason said.

"Maybe there's another entrance?" Lizzy said, looking to the side.

Morty and Jason each picked a different direction and walked along the castle wall, looking up and down for an entrance. Lizzy studied the door and noticed details she hadn't seen at first. Etched in the ice were vines and leaves. A huge curtain of frozen ivy stretched all the way to the ground. She could see a large hole in the center of the ivy. Lizzy stepped forward and edged her fingers into the hole.

"Hey, I think this might be a keyhole," she called out to the others.

Jason and Morty joined her and peered at the hole.

"Looks like a skeleton key fits in it. But we don't have the key." Jason said. "Can you get one from your sack, Morty?"

"I can try," he said and began rummaging inside his sack. "Give me a hand, would you, Jason? It's heavy."

Jason reached down into the sack and helped Morty lift out a giant brass key. Together they fit it into the keyhole and tried to turn it. The key didn't budge.

"Can you give me a boost again, Morty? This time we'll use your branches." Jason said. "Maybe I can use my weight to turn it?"

Morty picked Jason up, and he grabbed the key at the top. Slowly Morty let go and left Jason hanging from the key. Nothing happened. Morty reached up and helped Jason down. Together, they pulled the big key out of the hole and dragged it off to the side.

Lizzy began walking, studying the various sculptures.

"Hey, where ya going?" Jason asked and jogged up to her.

"I'm just looking." They both walked, zigzagging around sculptures and trees. "It's like a maze or a puzzle. That means there's got to be a solution somewhere in here."

Lizzy stopped. "This is funny, take a look at this!"

Jason walked over to stand beside her and squinted, trying to figure out what she meant. After a moment, he said, "It kinda looks like a foot, don't you think?"

She reached out a hand to touch the ice. A fine coating of ice crystals clung to her glove, as she ran her hand along it. "It feels bumpy."

Jason reached out and felt along the ice. "You're right. It kinda feels like... scales." Lizzy took a couple steps back and looked up. Above her were two giant wings, swooped as though landing. Huge talons hung above them, light glinting off the sharp tips.

"Oh, Jason, it's a dragon!" Lizzy said, her voice squeaky

with fear and surprise. "It's so pretty!" They walked a bit further back to get a better view.

"Morty, come check this out. We found a dragon ice sculpture," Jason yelled.

Morty hopped up beside them. "Oh my, goodness me," Morty cried and tumbled backward. "It's so big. And fierce looking." If he hadn't been made of snow, Jason was sure Morty would have shivered in fear.

Lizzy gave a sharp cry and ran forward.

"What's wrong?" Jason cried, running after her. She climbed over the extended foot until she was up against the dragon's exposed belly and directly under its talons.

"Look, Jason, it's holding something!" she cried. "It looks like a key. Morty, can you lift me up? I think I can get it out."

Morty hesitated. "Are you sure it's… safe?" he asked.

Lizzy nodded. Morty hopped over to Lizzy and lifted her toward the claws above them.

"Turn me around, Morty, please. I need to get to the back of the claws."

Morty slowly turned and put his back to the dragon. "Please hurry. I've got a bad feeling about this."

"What? Why??" Jason asked, watching his sister as she

slowly pulled the heavy key out of its narrow space. It looked like a giant block of ice carved into the shape of a skeleton key.

Morty lowered Lizzy to the ground. "Because it looks a bit too much like the ice dragon for my taste. That's not a creature you want to have mad at you."

"Come on. Let's go try it, and see if it works." Jason and Lizzy ran back the way they came, as Morty hopped along behind them. Morty lifted Lizzy who put the key into the hole. It didn't turn but went all the way forward until the entire key fit inside the hole. As they watched, it vanished into the door.

"Oh no!" Lizzy cried. "It's gone!"

Jason groaned and Morty slowly lowered Lizzy to the ground.

After a moment, the door gave a mighty series of crackles and icy screeches, then slid open.

CHAPTER TEN

All three stepped through the door into a clear courtyard. Nothing was in sight as they started across the empty landscape with ice crunching beneath their feet. There was a strange hush all around them, not even the wind seemed able to blow. There were no birds, no animal sounds, just the sharp sounds of breaking ice, loud as thunder in their ears. Lizzy held Jason's hand tight.

They came to a series of icy steps and another smaller door. This one opened at a simple touch, swinging inward noiselessly. They entered a shadowy hallway. Every few feet, ice sculptures decorated both sides of the hallway. The silence and the cold combined to feel like a force of its own.

They turned a corner, and Morty hopped right into a giant ice sculpture. It towered above them. Jagged, sharp chunks of ice stuck out in all directions. The creature moved as they watched. The arms bent, and the legs stretched forward as it moved toward them. The ice crackled as the sculpture bent down to look at them, brilliant eyes as red and bright as rubies. Morty stood, frozen in place.

"Run, Lizzy!" Jason cried and pulled her around back the way they'd come.

Jason's yell got Morty's attention. He hopped backward as the creature began to take a giant step toward them. When its leg crashed down, the floor vibrated beneath their feet.

Morty spun around and caught up to Jason and Lizzy. He grabbed them and hopped harder than he'd ever hopped before. Still, the golem chased after them. It gave a mighty roar that reached into their bones and filled them with terror. The very walls seemed to tremble. They reached another corner, and Morty slid around it.

Running toward them in giant leaping strides was another ice creature. Jason and Lizzy screamed as Morty struggled to stop. The ice was too slippery. He couldn't stop, so he turned his back toward the creature and held Jason and Lizzy in front of him to protect them. Morty's slide began to slow, and then with a small bump, he finally came to a stop. Morty turned to look behind him. He had come to rest against the ice creature's frozen foot. Carefully, he set the children on their feet, as the other creature came up behind them.

"We're boxed in," Jason whispered to Morty. "Got anything in your magic sack for this?"

"Like what?" Morty looked at Jason. "They're made of ice!"

"How about a torch?" Jason asked.

"No weapons remember? Plus, how would I light it?"

"Think of a lighter," Jason said, getting impatient.

"You want me to think with those two things ready to crush us?" Morty reached for his sack anyway as Jason edged closer to his sister and pulled her to his side, holding her close. Before Morty could open it, the ice creature reached down a giant arm and snatched the bag away. The other golem yanked the picnic basket from Lizzy's hands.

"Hey," she cried, trying to hold on. "That's not yours!"

"Give it back," Jason yelled.

The creature growled at Lizzy then gestured for them to move forward. Together, the creatures herded the party down the narrow hallway and into an empty, windowless room. One golem raised his hands over the trio. Lizzy and Jason clung to each other, shaking in terror. Morty tried to shield the children with his snowy body.

Large icicles rained down all around them, thudding into the ground and knocking Jason and Lizzy off their feet. Lizzy stared up at the golems who turned and marched back out, stomping down the hallway. She looked around them. Giant icicles towered around them. Small spaces showed between them. She walked forward and tried to reach her hand through the opening. The ice crackled and shifted toward her hand. Lizzy snatched it back before the ice could trap her fingers. As her hand drew away, the ice withdrew, leaving a gap.

"We're trapped." Jason pulled his knees up to his chest.

Morty looked around in panic.

"Maybe we can climb out?" Lizzy suggested.

Jason stepped closer to the icicles and ran his glove down it. It came away slick with ice. "I don't think so. It's too slippery."

Lizzy walked the full perimeter of their cage. After twenty steps, she returned to the place she started from.

"This is bad," Morty cried. "This is so bad. What are we going to do? There's not going to be any Christmas, the Snowman Village is going to be melted forever, and we're trapped in Jack Frost's castle with no hope of escaping."

Lizzy walked over to Morty. "Morty, it'll be okay. You'll see. We just can't give up."

"And it's all my fault," Morty wailed and hung his snowy head. Tiny ice crystals fell toward the floor.

Lizzy bit her lip and thought, *Oh boy. Just what we need, a freaked out snowman.*

"Don't worry, Morty," Jason said, trying to sound confident. "I'm sure someone will rescue us."

"Not in time to save Christmas. It's almost sunset on Christmas Eve. They'll never get here in time!"

Jason and Lizzy looked at each other. Neither spoke. There wasn't anything they could say to reassure him. Morty continued to weep tiny snowflakes into a pile at their feet. Jason and Lizzy clasped hands and sat on the icy ground to wait for whatever was going to happen next.

❄ ❄ ❄ ❄ ❄

As Jason and Lizzy tried to think of a way to escape, the golems marched deeper into the castle's center. After many twists and turns, they arrived at a giant chamber. Delicate icicles dangled from a high domed ceiling. They clinked together like chimes and echoed through the room. In the center was a chair carved completely out of ice. In it was a person who appeared human, yet no human could have sat on such an icy throne. It was none other than Jack Frost.

"Yes, yes, what is it?" He glared at the creatures as they stopped and knelt.

"We captured two prisoners, Your Iciness. They are in the anteroom near where we found them snooping. They tried to run but we caught them. They had this." The golem handed the picnic basket and sack to Jack Frost.

"A snowman's sack?" Jack held it up before him. "And just what do you think I could do with this? Put ice cubes in it?" He tossed the bag aside and rolled his eyes, then lifted up the lid of the picnic basket.

"Now, what's this?" He picked up the small package inside. Wrapped in blue wrapping paper with a silver bow etched with snowflakes, as Jack turned the package, the snowflakes looked like they were falling.

"Isn't that clever?" He turned the package and spotted a little tag in the shape of a miniature Christmas present. Written on it were the words: "For Jack, Merry Christmas."

Jack looked up at the golem. "Where did you get this? Did the snowman give you this?"

"No, King of Ice. The snowman only had the sack. The children had the basket."

"Children?" Jack Frost stood. "Here? Where?"

"We put them in an icicle cage in the anteroom."

"Did you make a mess again?" Jack bellowed. "How many times have I told you not to throw your ice around?"

"We're sorry, Your Iciness. We needed to secure the prisoners."

"They're not prisoners, you giant, dumb hunk of ice." Jack sighed. "Bring the children to me. I don't have any need for the snowman." Jack glared at them and pointed. "And you better clean up that mess, or you'll be sleeping outside the boundary. I hear it's much warmer there than in here. Maybe a little melting would help you remember."

"As you wish, Master of Winter," the golems bowed then stomped back out the way they had come.

"Oh, for flying snowflakes, they're worse than children," Jack groaned and leaned his head onto his hand.

Jack picked up the small package, looking at the shiny silver bow. Jack's brow furrowed into lines as he puzzled why anyone would give him a present. He hadn't received a Christmas present since that long-ago day when his mother died.

He could still remember the day as though he'd just lived it, even though countless Christmases had passed. A crackling fire danced and crackled in the fireplace. Three bright red stockings hung from the mantle. A modest Christmas tree sparkled with lights, presents piled high beneath the tree. In a rocking chair, a little boy sat on the lap of a beautiful lady. She read a Christmas story aloud, her auburn hair swept back in a half ponytail, and her mouth curled in a smile. Jack could almost smell her and feel the warmth of her arms as he remembered the story.

The door to the chamber swung open, and the golems returned, two children walking between them, holding hands. Jack watched as they stopped a short distance from the giant ice throne and stood shivering in the icy, cold chamber. Even their winter clothes weren't enough to keep them warm in such a freezing place.

CHAPTER ELEVEN

Lizzy stared at the throne. Jack Frost was very thin like a willow tree. He almost looked like a strong wind would blow him over. He wasn't much taller than an average human. His skin was very pale and his hair was pure white like freshly fallen snow.

"What brings you here?" Jack Frost asked, then stood and walked the three short steps to them. He circled, observing them as they tried to follow his movement.

Lizzy's teeth began to chatter in the silence and cold. "We wanted t-t-to wish you a Merry Christmas, M-M-Mr. Frost."

"Wish me a Merry Christmas?" Jack looked surprised. "Is it that time already? It must have slipped my mind."

Lizzy looked up at him with wide eyes, as though the idea had never occurred to her.

Jack held up the small box. "And this? Did you bring this as well?"

"Yes, sir," Lizzy replied and reached out to hug her brother close for warmth.

"And just why would you do such a thing?"

"B-b-b-because it's C-C-Christmas," Lizzy said through her chattering teeth.

Jack turned away from them and stroked his chin thoughtfully then turned back. "Yes? And?"

Lizzy stopped and thought for a moment. "Sir, my Mom says Christmas is a time for Christmas spirit, and to give gifts to others. We wanted you to have one too."

Jack stood silent for a long time.

Lizzy hesitated. "Won't you open it and see what it is?"

Jack looked at the package in his hand as if the thought hadn't occurred to him. He looked at Lizzy then back at the present. "Alright, why not?"

Jack yanked the end of the bow to unravel it then tore the paper from the package. He lifted the lid and stared. Lizzy could see nestled in colorful red and green tissue paper were the frosted cookies she and Mrs. Claus had carefully made, each one a different shape with colored icing. Inside laid a Christmas tree shaped cookie decorated with red ornaments and a bright yellow star on top. Another looked like a red Christmas ornament. Jack lifted a cookie in the shape of a red and white striped candy cane and held it before him, gazing in wonder. Each stripe was perfect, and the cookie almost looked too good to eat.

He brought the cookie to his mouth and took a bite. Lizzy held her breath and squeezed Jason tight. Jack's eyes drifted closed as he chewed. Jack opened his eyes and looked at Lizzy.

"What do you think, Mr. Frost?" Lizzy spoke in a soft voice and tried to keep her voice from shaking. "I helped make them. I did the icing and everything."

Jack took a big bite, and then another until the cookie was gone.

Jack stepped forward and kneeled to look Lizzy in the eye. In a gentle voice filled with awe, he asked, "Why in all that is snowy would you decide to bring me Christmas cookies? No one gives me anything for Christmas, not even a Christmas card, other than Santa. Or even a thank you for bringing the snow for the season."

"Well," Lizzy hesitated then swallowed. "Mrs. Claus said she remembered you liked frosted sugar cookies, and we all decided to make you some, to wish you a Merry Christmas."

Jason nodded then said, "We just moved to Texas from Chicago this year; and for the first time, we haven't had snow before Christmas." He stopped for a moment. "I never realized how much I like snow until I couldn't go sledding or have a snowball fight. Or how much it makes Christmas better.

Morty agreed. "We really want to thank you for bringing the winter every year."

Jack smiled a big smile. "Ah, appreciation. That's as good of a gift as the cookies. It does take a great deal of work, you know."

Lizzy thought hard for a moment. "You're always working to undo the melting caused by the sun, aren't you?"

"It's hard work to keep it cold enough that the snow doesn't melt away. This is my busiest time of the year."

Jack stood, and Lizzy noticed his ears turned just a little pink, as though embarrassed by their praise. "But enough about that. This is no place for children. Let's get you two home, shall we?"

"Wait," Lizzy said, reaching out to touch Jack's arm. She ignored the iciness that coursed through her fingertips. "If it's okay, we actually need to go to Santa's workshop first."

"Santa's workshop?" Jack stared at Lizzy. "I haven't been there in years. But why do you need to go there first?"

Lizzy told Jack about their wish for snow, how they met Morty, their visit to Mother Nature's tree, and how they came to find his castle.

Jack Frost was silent for a long time. Lizzy's chattering teeth echoed in the empty hall. Jason's teeth began to chatter as well. "Sir, would you happen to have anything we could get warm with? P-p-please? My sister and I are very c-c-cold."

Jack walked over to the red sack lying near the throne. "I believe this belongs to you?" Jason took the bag and closed his eyes. He reached his arm into the sack and began to pull out an enormous blanket. He pulled and pulled and pulled some more. It was bright red and thick. He wrapped himself and his sister tightly in the blanket.

"How'd you do that?" Lizzy asked.

"I just pretended we were camping and toasting marshmallows and thought how nice it would be to cuddle up in a warm blanket." Jason shrugged.

"Great idea Jason!" Lizzy said, impressed. "I never would have thought of that."

Jack looked at Lizzy for a long time. He stroked his chin. Then he looked at the cookies sitting in their box on the arm of his chair.

"It sounds like you're in need of a nice, winter blizzard for a few days. That should stop the village from melting. At least until Mother Nature gets back and fixes her weather machine."

"Oh, that would be fantastic." Lizzy grinned. "We sure could use the help."

Jack nodded. "All right, it's settled then. Now, let's see about your snowy friend, and be on our way."

CHAPTER TWELVE

Frost led the way through the halls until they reached a very frantic Morty. His scarf looked almost unraveled as he sat in the center of the ice cage. An ice golem stepped forward and removed two of the giant icicles. Morty peered out, uncertain, until he saw Jason and Lizzy.

"Oh my goodness, thank heavens you're both all right…" He stopped as Jack Frost came into view. "And you, sir, have held us against our will. You should be ashamed."

Jack smiled at Morty. "Now, now, no need to be testy. We don't get many visitors here, as you can imagine."

"I should think not if this is how you treat them."

Jack laughed and gestured for them to follow him. "True, true, Mr. Snowman. Now, I understand time is running out for your village. We should get going, don't you think?"

Morty began to hop toward Jason and Lizzy but stopped at Jack's words. "What?" He looked at Jason and Lizzy. "What does he mean, 'going?'"

Jason smiled at Morty, "Jack's going to help us."

Lizzy nodded, her eyes sparkling.

"Well, I will be a snowstorm! That's wonderful!" Morty looked as relieved as a snowman could look. "I guess Christmas miracles still do happen."

The group rounded a corner and arrived at a giant double door. With a wave of Jack's hand, the door slid open, revealing a cavernous room. Blue ice stretched in all directions. In the middle of the room rested a giant wooden airship. The hull was a deep reddish color of rich mahogany. A carved image of a dragon formed the ship's prow. The ship reminded Lizzy of home and she swallowed. She missed home, her bed, and her toys. She missed her mom and dad. Their adventure had been fun but she really just wanted to curl up on her mommy's lap, listen to a story, and fall asleep to the sound of her voice.

"Are we going to ride in that?" Jason asked.

Jack beamed and held out a hand toward the ship. "Welcome to the 'Winter Voyager.' I built her myself." He led the way to a detachable staircase, and soon everyone was aboard—even Morty, although he needed some help from the ice golems.

A team of miniature ice golems, similar to the larger guardian ice creatures, scurried around the deck. They set up the rigging, unfurled the sails, and prepared to leave. Overhead, Lizzy could see a double bay of doors begin to swing outward. The ship rose through the air, cleared the doors and turned toward the North Pole. With the barest movement, the ship began to glide noiselessly through the air.

"Mr. Frost?" Lizzy asked. "Why is your ship made out of wood and not ice, like everything else?"

Jack chuckled and rubbed a nearby railing. "Because wood is just as beautiful as ice. Ice is hard and strong, but wood is beautiful in its own way. It's soft and yielding. It reminds me of my childhood."

"Wow," Jason leaned over a side railing next to Frost at the helm and looked behind them. "How does it work?"

"The sails capture the air to move us forward." Jack winked at Jason. "A little touch of magic doesn't hurt either."

Lizzy watched as they sailed through puffy, white clouds. Ice crystals sparkled off the frozen trail in the sunlight behind them. One cloud passed close enough, Lizzy reached out a hand to touch it. She laughed when her hand came away wet. The clouds began to turn into ice, and snow fell as the ship drew away.

"Hey Jason, look! We're making it snow." They stood side by side, watching the snow falling behind them.

Jason looked at Lizzy. "I bet Mom is going to be really mad at us for not coming home for lunch."

Lizzy bit her lip. "Yeah, we're probably going to be grounded."

Jason sighed and leaned his chin on his arms. "And we can't even tell her we saved Christmas."

"She wouldn't believe you anyway," Morty said from behind them. "Most adults forget what it means to believe in Santa and Christmas."

Lizzy turned toward Jack, frowning. "We won't forget, will we?"

Jack laughed. "That all depends on you. If you believe in your heart and remember what the meaning of Christmas truly is, then you will always carry Christmas spirit within you. It's hard to forget that once you've found it."

The ship began to edge lower and came to rest on a deep snow bank not far from Santa's workshop. Mrs. Claus hurried toward them. Lizzy went down the ladder first.

Mrs. Claus gave Lizzy a tight hug, then Jason. She looked at Jack. "Oh, thank goodness! We were so worried when Hot Rod came back without them."

"Hello, Mrs. Claus."

"Welcome to the North Pole, Jack." Mrs. Claus gave him a warm hug then led them inside. "It's been too long since you've visited. Come with me. Santa's in the workshop and almost ready for tonight's deliveries."

Santa's workshop was abuzz with noisy machines, chattering excited elves, and various activities. Elves worked in rows, creating toys, applying final touches, and wrapping boxes with beautiful paper covered with miniature Santas. Each finished box had a colorful bow and a tag. A long line of elves passed the finished gifts up to Santa, who tucked them into his huge red sack.

As they followed Mrs. Claus, elves nudged one another and pointed at them. Whispers rose up through the workshop as elves stopped and stared. Lizzy could see one of the elves tap Santa's arm and cup a hand to yell in his ear. Santa turned from what he was doing and hurried toward them, Gary and Jonah right behind him.

"Ho Ho Ho! Why, Merry Christmas, Jack!" Santa boomed, smiling as he walked up and held out his hand for Jack to shake. "Good to see you, old friend."

"Santa, I thought you were mad at Jack?" Lizzy asked.

Santa knelt before Lizzy. "You know, Lizzy, at one time I was very angry. But you helped me realize I miss my dear friend more. I just couldn't seem to find a way to tell him I forgave him a long time ago. He made a mistake, and everyone makes them once in a while."

Santa stood and looked at Jack. "Can you forgive an old friend for being stubborn much too long?"

Jack looked down and tried to wipe away an icy tear without anyone noticing. "I think that's the most beautiful thing anyone has ever said to me. I hope you'll forgive me too, Santa. I'm sorry for not helping you with Christmas."

"It's all in the past, Jack," Santa clapped Jack on the shoulder. "Now, though, I have to finish getting ready for

Christmas. And I know two children who need to be tucked snug in their beds with visions of sugar plums dancing in their heads."

"Awww, Santa," Lizzy's shoulders drooped. "Can't we help you deliver Christmas presents?"

"Ho, Ho, Ho!" Santa threw his head back and laughed, holding his belly. "You've both helped to save Christmas. Why don't you leave the deliveries to me?"

Jason put his arm around Lizzy's shoulders. "Come on, Sis. Let's go home."

Lizzy wanted to cry. Now that it was over, Lizzy almost didn't want to go. She would miss all her new friends but couldn't wait to be home again. "Home does sound really good."

Santa and Mrs. Claus walked with them back to Jack's ship and gave them both a hug.

"What about us?" Gary asked. "How are we going to get home?"

Everyone stopped to look at Gary and Jonah.

Santa's eyes twinkled. "Ah, yes, we can't forget the two who started this whole mess. What should we do with them?"

"We could make them walk back to Mother Nature's

tree," offered Morty, still upset over the Snowman Village's close call.

"Oh, no, please don't do that," Gary shuddered, making his feathers rustle. "I'm not made for ice and snow! Plus, after what happened last time…"

Everyone laughed.

"Jack?" Jonah waddled forward a few steps. "Could you possibly give us a lift to Mother Nature's tree in your airship? We're a bit stranded at present."

"I don't know," Jack replied, "From how I understand it, you two have created quite a mess. Maybe a nice walk would help you remember not to do it again."

"Oh no sir, we've learned our lesson," Jonah cried, flapping his flippers and shuffling in a small circle.

"We won't ever touch Mother Nature's weather machine without permission again," Gary added. Jonah nodded hard in agreement with each word. "We promise!"

"Well," Jack paused and looked at Lizzy. "What do you think?"

Lizzy tilted her head and put a finger on her chin as if deep in thought. "If they're really sorry…"

"Oh we are," Gary and Jonah interrupted. "We swear, we are so, so, so sorry."

"… and they promise to never do it again…" Jason added, grinning along with his sister.

"They did do a lot to help out at the workshop," Santa added.

"Pretty please?" Jonah begged, shuffling his feet.

Everyone laughed and Lizzy said. "Then yes, I think they should be able to go home too."

Jack held out an arm toward the ship. "Alright then, welcome aboard. After you."

Gary and Jonah looked at the ship towering above him and the rope ladder dangling from the side then back at Jack. "You're joking, right?"

Jack laughed. He and Santa helped both birds up onto the deck. Jason and Lizzy followed them and stood at the railing. Santa and Mrs. Claus waved from the ground as the ship rose into the sky and began the trip to Morty's village.

CHAPTER THIRTEEN

It was a short trip and Lizzy slept through almost all of it. When she woke, the airship began to descend. She and Jason rushed to a railing and watched the ship come to rest in a snow bank. The snowmen came forward, hopping slowly. Each one varied in size and shape. Some were fat, some were skinny, some were tall, and some were short. Several smaller snowmen were obviously children. They all looked just a bit mushy. Several had droopy faces with crooked noses or arms hung limp at their sides. Obviously, some of them had started melting.

As the snowmen came closer to the airship, Lizzy heard one of them yell, "It's colder! It's getting colder!"

Together, the snowmen hopped faster toward the cooler air. Jack Frost appeared at the helm of the airship, and Morty joined him. Morty's snow sparkled like the freshest snow ever to fall as he beamed down at his friends. "Jack Frost has come to help us! He's going to make it cold again!"

With that, Jack Frost drew in a deep breath, sounding like a huge suction hose, and then carefully blew. A sparkly blue cloud flew from his lips and began to spread forward, growing bigger. Snow glimmered and sparkled as it began to fall on everything the cloud touched. The snowmen turned their faces up and watched as the snow fell, coating them. Several closed their eyes in relief. Snowmen cheered as their exteriors began to get firmer. Snowmen straightened scarves and limbs and adjusted their crooked noses into their proper places. Children hopped around their parents, tossing snow into the air with shouts of glee. "Yay, there will be Christmas."

Morty, Jason, Lizzy, and Jack Frost descended a gangplank, and the snowmen gathered around them. Many hugged Morty, babbling all at once, asking him all about his adventure. Others stared at Jack Frost in awe, from a distance. Lizzy could tell, for many, many Christmases to come there would be tales about how Morty helped save the Snowman Village.

An older snowman came forward, holding onto an icy cane. He stopped in front of Jack. "We owe you a debt, great frost-bringer. How can we ever repay you?"

Jack smiled at the short, chubby snowman before him. "Your thanks are enough. And a Merry Christmas to all of you."

"We most certainly thank you. And to celebrate, you must join us for our winter festival. There's dancing and beautiful music as we pay a tribute to winter, Christmas, and all the joys the season brings. In fact, you are invited every year from now on."

Lizzy and Jason looked at Jack.

Jack hesitated. "You want me? At your festival?"

The snowman elder nodded. "You would be our guest of honor. It would allow us to thank you properly."

"I've never been invited to a festival to celebrate winter before." Jack smiled and his eyes danced. "Of course, I'd be delighted to join you!"

The snowmen cheered as snow continued to fall in a light shower of snowflakes.

As promised, later that evening, there was a great ceremony with dancing, singing, laughter, and frozen treats. Jason and Lizzy huddled in their red blanket, watching and laughing as the snowmen danced around Jack, showering him with snow. Jack stood, a little uncertain, but smiling nonetheless. Jason and Lizzy sipped hot cocoa and nibbled on sandwiches.

Morty hopped up to them. "It's getting late. We have a bed ready for you."

They followed him into a nearby house, carved from snow and ice. In the center of the large room was a bed covered with blankets and pillows.

"Is this your house, Morty?" Lizzy asked and yawned so hard her jaw popped.

Morty tucked the covers around Jason and Lizzy. "It sure is."

"Morty?" Lizzy said.

"Yes, dear one."

"Will you stay with us for a while?"

Morty smiled. "Of course."

❄ ❄ ❄ ❄ ❄

It wasn't long before Jason and Lizzy were sound asleep, Lizzy cuddled up to her big brother, and Jason with his arm around her. Morty stood nearby, watching over them both. Jack Frost joined him. "It's time."

"Yes." Morty sighed. Small snowflakes floated to the floor. "I'm really going to miss them."

Jack patted Morty on the back then stepped closer to the two sleeping children. He gently blew frost over them. Morty and Jack watched as the frost drifted through the air to settle on Jason and Lizzy. "Merry Christmas and thank you both for your many gifts."

Their bodies began to shimmer and fade away until they had disappeared.

"Do you think we'll ever see them again?" Morty asked.

"Only time will tell," Jack said. They stood there, staring at the empty bed in the darkness for a long time.

❄ ❄ ❄ ❄ ❄

With Jason, Lizzy, and Morty taken care of, Jack returned to the airship the next morning and headed for Mother Nature's tree.

Jack finally landed the ship next to Mother Nature's tree. Curled up on the far side of the deck, Gary and Jonah were enjoying a midday nap. Gary gave the occasional snort and shook his feathers, lost in a dream.

"Rise and shine, boys," Jack said.

Gary and Jonah opened their eyes and looked up at Jack. "Are we there yet?"

Jack chuckled then nodded. Still sleepy, they stepped onto a nearby branch and made their way into the house. Inside, birds flew here and there, singing sweet music in time with their wing beats.

"Mother Nature must have returned," Jonah said, looking around. "The birds only sing when she's around."

"Uh oh," Gary replied and huddled behind Jonah. "And here she comes now. And with Father Time, too."

"She doesn't look very happy, does she?" Jonah asked, looking at Jack, who only shrugged.

"Where on earth have you two been?" Mother Nature said and put a hand on her hip. "And what have you done to the weather machine?"

"It was an accident, Mother—" Jonah started.

Mother Nature didn't pause to let him finish. "You two have so much explaining to do. I am especially curious about why the tree was filled with sand."

"Well," Gary offered. "First there was a rainbow and hail then a sandstorm."

"A sandstorm?" Mother Nature cried and threw up her hands. "How many times have I told you not to ever, ever touch the weather machine? What do I have to do? Put you in a timeout or something?"

Jack looked amused. "You know, Mother, I think we may have a lot in common there, but you might have it much worse than I do with my ice golems."

"You have no idea." Mother Nature grumbled, glaring at the two humbled birds then sighed. "Come on you two, I'm just glad you're both okay. You can explain what happened over lunch."

❄ ❄ ❄ ❄ ❄

As the sun rose on that crisp sunny Christmas day, Lizzy and Jason opened their eyes and looked at each other. Lizzy sat up and looked around.

"Where are we?" Lizzy asked, confused.

"In my room, silly." Jason stood and stretched. "Come on, let's go see what Mom's making for breakfast."

"But Jason, weren't we in Morty's house?"

"It's Christmas morning, silly." Jason frowned. "Wait, that wasn't a dream?"

Lizzy shook her head. "No, I was there. We didn't have the same dream – it was real."

"So, you mean we really went to the North Pole and met Santa?"

"Yep."

"But how did we get here?" Jason asked.

Lizzy stopped and thought. "Magic, I guess."

"Come on, let's go downstairs." Jason threw back the covers. "Mom and Dad are gonna be worried sick."

They ran down the stairs and into the kitchen. Their mother stood, cupping a steaming cup of coffee, and leaning against the kitchen counter.

Father, sitting at the kitchen table, put down his newspaper. "There you two are. We wondered if you were going to sleep all day. Did you forget it's Christmas?"

Lizzy looked at Jason, and neither could think of what to say. They turned and ran into the living room. The Christmas tree lights twinkled, and light sparkled on silver tinsel. Christmas presents covered the floor. Two presents stood out from the rest for Jason and Lizzy.

Lizzy pointed and whispered to Jason, "Look, Jason, its Santa's wrapping paper."

Their parents joined them. "Well, what are you waiting for? Let's open some presents!"

Jason and Lizzy went straight for the two presents wrapped in Santa's special wrapping paper. Jason opened his present first and pulled a small yellow airplane out of the box.

Lizzy tore the paper away from hers and gently lifted the lid and laughed. She held it up for her brother to see. "Jason, look its Morty!" They both laughed, Lizzy gave him a big hug, then they ran to show their parents. Outside, a light snow fell.

THE END

(Or is it?)

ACKNOWLEDGEMENTS

Writing a book is more than a lone author typing away for hours at a keyboard into the wee hours of the night. It starts very simply in most cases. This book was born while sitting at our kitchen table over the Thanksgiving holiday, waiting on a pumpkin pie to finish cooking. We were role-playing with kids. One thing led to another and through a great deal of encouragement and help, the book you hold was finished after two years of effort.

I have written this, first, for my daughter Libby. Without her, this book could not exist. Libby is the inspiration behind Lizzy's character and while they are completely different, they are similar in their sweet innocence. Libby also actively participated in the planning for book two, *Jason Lizzy & the Ice Dragon*.

Next, I wrote this book because, quite simply, I had a blast coming up with the characters and scenarios. I fell in love with the whole project and spent numerous hours batting around ideas, arguing over characters and plot, and trying to tell a story with meaning and holiday spirit.

Lastly, but most importantly, I wrote this for my audience. To help children, young and old, to remember the joy of the Christmas season, the meaning behind it, and to share a little bit of love and inspiration. I hope reading this book delights you as much as I was delighted to create it!

SPECIAL THANKS

❇ David Duhr of Write by Night for his expertise, encouragement, and being my accountability partner throughout the first draft. His support made all the difference in me completing this overwhelming project, the first of many more to come (hopefully).

❇ My editor, Margo Dill, whose attention to detail and perspective helped me raise the book's quality immeasurable levels. She caught all the large and small mistakes so you, dear reader, would not have to. That being said, any mistakes that may remain, are completely my fault.

❇ Jillian Dodd, Nigel Blackwell, and Mary Morgan for their patience, encouragement, support and most importantly, alleviating my paralyzing fear about self-publishing. Win, lose, or draw, this book probably would have never seen the light of day beyond my hard drive without all of your help and support. I could not ask for better friends and fellow writers.

❄ I cannot forget Skip Yelle, a.k.a. Dad. Words cannot adequately describe my love for you. You have never stopped believing in me, even when I stopped believing in myself or just wanted to give up. Through all my struggles, joys, and setbacks, you have never wavered. Your love, patience and support has changed my life in uncountable ways and I will be forever grateful. Everything I write and publish is only possible because you saw potential in a young woman just entering adulthood and nurtured that potential into success even after countless others turned away. You filled the void in my life and raised me into the woman I have become, even though it wasn't your responsibility to do so. No greater gift can be given than unselfish love and I hope one day to make a similar difference to another person in this world as you have for me. I hope you know how incredible you are and how blessed I am to have you in my life. I love you always and forever.

❄ To Mikey Brooks, who helped to bring new life to the front cover. You are an extremely talented artist to have been able to understand my vision so well. I am humbled by your generosity, your support and your devotion to perfection.

❄ I could devote an entire book to thanking the countless people who had a role, even minor, in this book's completion. Since I'm limited on space, I've highlighted the people who played a pivotal role in the project with special words of thanks. However, I also want to thank our friends and beta readers for their selfless support. Thanks for listening to our endless strategizing and ad nauseam story details. In addition, to the countless strangers who struck up conversations with me and found themselves curiously intrigued by my shameless mentioning of the book. You know who you are. We appreciate you too!

ABOUT THE AUTHOR

Charity Marie has been writing for over 25 years. She is also mother to two children. She writes children's books (which surprises her daily), fiction of all kinds, nonfiction, and occasionally a little poetry.

Originally, from Florida, she is proud to call Texas home. When she is not busy with her many interests and responsibilities, she is a consumer advocate, poker aficionado and player, avid reader and reviewer, gamer and faithful CSI fan. Charity is easy to connect with online or off. She loves to hear from her readers and can be contacted through the various methods below.

Email: authorcharitymarie@gmail.com

Facebook: https://www.facebook.com/AuthorCharityMarie/

Website: www.charitymarie.com

Goodreads: http://www.goodreads.com/CharityKountz

Available now in print and eBook!

Jason and Lizzy embark on another exciting quest, this time to restore Mother Nature's balance and protect her tree from the Ice Dragon. Book two is their wildest adventure yet! Also, joining them are beloved characters Jonah the penguin and Gary the turkey among other new friends. Visit www.charitymarie.com for the next adventure!

www.ingramcontent.com/pod-product-compliance
Lightning Source LLC
LaVergne TN
LVHW091601060526
838200LV00036B/944